WELSH
RECIPES

Traditional Welsh Fare
Bwyd Traddodiadol o Gymru

SALMON

Index

Cover pictures: *front:* Llanberis Pass *back:* Carew Castle
title page: In the Black Mountains by Sutton Palmer

Printed and Published by Dorrigo, Manchester, England. © Copyright.

Snowdon Pudding
Pwdin Eryri

Named after Wales's highest mountain, this steamed marmalade pudding is surmounted by a summit of raisins.

2 oz. raisins	Grated rind of 2 lemons
4 oz. suet	1½ oz. ground rice or cornflour
Pinch of salt	3 oz. soft brown sugar
4 oz. fresh breadcrumbs	3 eggs
3 oz. lemon marmalade	

Butter a 1 pint pudding basin. Cover the base with the raisins. Mix all the dry ingredients together in a bowl. Beat the eggs and add to the mixture with the marmalade. Pour the mixture into the basin and cover with greaseproof paper and kitchen foil. Steam for 1½ hours topping up the water as necessary. Serve hot with custard. Serves 4.

Manorbier Castle near Tenby by A. de Breanski Jnr.

Laverbread Cakes
Teisennau Bara Lawr

Laver is a red-coloured edible seaweed that grows on rocks around the Welsh coast. For these cakes it is mixed with oatmeal and fried with bacon, for breakfast.

**1 lb. laverbread   4 oz. fine oatmeal
6 rashers bacon**

Mix the laverbread and oatmeal together and form the mixture into small, round, flatish cakes. Fry the prepared cakes in hot fat (preferably bacon fat) using a palette knife to keep them in shape. Fry until they are crisp and brown on both sides. Serve with the grilled rashers of bacon as a breakfast dish.

Prepared laver, usually tinned, can be obtained from health food shops, specialist grocers or some supermarkets. If bought fresh it must be washed VERY well in cold, running water to remove all sand and then boiled in water for 30 to 40 minutes and drained thoroughly; at this stage it will look a little like cooked spinach. When cooked it is minced or chopped and it then becomes laverbread, ready for use.

Welsh Leek Broth
Cawl Cennin

There are a number of versions of this broth. Sometimes it would be thickened with oatmeal, sometimes it would be sieved before serving and sometimes a piece of bacon would be included, to be eaten separately as a main course after the broth had been served. Any left over broth was reheated for use the next day, when it was known as Cawl Eildwym; "twice heated broth".

1 oz. butter
6 leeks, washed, trimmed and cut
   into 1 inch pieces
3 medium potatoes, peeled and cubed

1 carrot, peeled and cubed (optional)
1 to 1½ pints chicken stock or water
Salt and black pepper
1 to 1½ pints milk

1 dessertspoon chopped fresh parsley

Melt the butter in a saucepan and sweat the vegetables gently until soft but not brown. Add the stock or water and seasoning, bring to the boil and simmer, covered, for 30 minutes until the vegetables are tender. Add the milk and heat thoroughly, but do not allow to boil. Stir in the parsley and serve in bowls, accompanied by crusty bread. If desired, the broth can be served sprinkled with grated cheese or snippets of crisply fried bacon. Serves 4 to 6.

Monmouth Stew
Stiw Mynwy

In Wales, lamb has always been a popular ingredient for stews and casseroles and this recipe contains leeks and pearl barley.

1½ lb. stewing lamb, cubed or 8 lamb chops, trimmed
1 oz. seasoned flour
1 oz. butter or oil
4 to 6 leeks, washed, trimmed and cut into rings

2 oz. pearl barley
4 sprigs of parsley, 1 sprig of thyme and a bayleaf, tied together with a piece of string
Salt and black pepper
¾ to 1 pint lamb stock

Set oven to 350°F or Mark 4. Coat the lamb in the seasoned flour, heat the butter or oil and lightly fry all over for 1 minute. Add the leeks and fry for a further minute, then transfer to a casserole dish. Add the pearl barley, herbs and seasoning, then pour over the stock. Cover, bring to the boil and cook in the oven for 1½ to 2 hours. Remove the herbs before serving and serve with boiled potatoes. Serves 4.

Alternatively, if desired, the stew can be cooked gently, covered, on top of the stove.

Welsh Salt Duck
Hwyaden Hallt Gymreig

This recipe appeared in 'The First Principles of Good Cookery' compiled in 1867.
Salt Duck has a very fresh taste.

1 large fresh, prepared duck, approximately 3½ to 4 lb. in weight,
purchased two days before required
6 oz. sea salt

Wipe the duck, then rub, inside and out with a quarter of the salt. Place on a large dish in the refrigerator. Later, repeat the process with a further quarter of the salt, turning the duck in any brine that has formed. The following day, repeat the process twice, using up the remainder of the salt. Next day, when the duck is due to be cooked, wash thoroughly, inside and out, under cold running water to remove all traces of salt. Set oven to 350°F or Mark 4. Pat the duck dry with kitchen paper, place in a casserole dish and just cover with water. Cover the casserole, place in pan of simmering water and cook for 1½ hours. Remove the duck from the casserole, drain very well and place in a baking tin. Increase oven to 450°F or Mark 8 and roast the duck for 20 to 30 minutes until the skin is crisp and golden. Serve with spinach and Onion or Laver and Orange Sauce. Serves 4.

Evening at Lake Vyrnwy by A. de Breanski Jnr.

Gwent Gooseberry Cream
Eirin Mair Hufennog Gwent

A South Wales recipe for poached gooseberries in a rich, creamy individual setting.

1 lb. gooseberries	**5 oz. plain yoghurt**
¾ oz. caster sugar	**A few drops vanilla essence**
8 oz. double cream	**1 teaspoon icing sugar**
6 dessertspoons demarara sugar	

Poach the gooseberries in a saucepan with a very little water and with the caster sugar; keep them whole by poaching gently and add more sugar if preferred. When cool, spoon the gooseberries, with a little juice, into 6 ramekin dishes. Beat the yoghurt and cream together until they form soft peaks, fold in the vanilla essence and icing sugar and spoon the mixture on top of the gooseberries. Sprinkle a dessert spoon of demarara sugar over the top of each ramekin. Cover with cling film and refrigerate for several hours. The sugar forms a nice crunchy topping. Serves 6.

Meat and Potatoes in the Oven
Tatws a Chig yn y Popty

This dish comes from North Wales and is particularly found in Anglesey.
Traditionally it is served with carrots or carrots and swedes mashed together.

2 to 2½ lb. breast of lamb, boned and rolled
1½ to 2 lb. potatoes, peeled, thickly sliced and weighed after preparation
½ oz. flour   Salt and black pepper
½ lb. onions, peeled, thickly sliced and weighed after preparation
½ to ¾ pint water or lamb stock

Set oven to 375°F or Mark 5. Place the lamb in a roasting tin and cook for 10 to 15 minutes. Remove the lamb and pour off any fat, leaving just a thin layer on the base of the tin. Cover the base of the tin with half the potatoes. Mix the flour and seasoning together and sprinkle over. Cover with the onion, top with the remainder of the potatoes and season well. Pour over the stock - it should come to just below the top layer of potatoes. Place the lamb on top, cover with a piece of kitchen foil and cook for 1½ to 1¾ hours, removing the foil for the last 10 to 15 minutes of cooking. Serve the lamb sliced, with the potatoes and onions and accompanied by carrots or mashed carrots and swede. Serve 4 to 6.

Criccieth Castle by Edwin Hayes

Welsh Faggots
Ffagodau Cymreig

These liver and onion balls are seasoned with sage and baked in stock, in the oven.

1 lb. pig's liver	**1 teaspoon fresh sage**
2 medium onions	**(or ½ teaspoon dried sage)**
3 oz. shredded suet	**Salt and pepper**
4 oz. fresh breadcrumbs	**½ pint beef stock**

Set oven to 350°F or Mark 4. Mince the liver and onion together, preferably in a food processor. Put into a bowl and stir in the suet, breadcrumbs, sage and seasoning to taste. Form the mixture into 12 balls with floured hands and place in a well greased, shallow ovenproof dish. Pour the stock into the dish. Cover and bake for about 30 minutes. Uncover and continue cooking for a further 10 minutes or so to brown the faggots. Remove the faggots from the dish and keep warm. The remaining gravy may then be thickened with cornflour or gravy browning, if preferred. Serve with creamed potatoes. Serves 6.

Fisherman's Stew
Stiw Pysgod

This recipe, which contains a variety of fish and shellfish, comes from the Gower.

2 pints cockles	**3 pints water**	**1 onion, quartered**	**½ teaspoon mace**
Salt and pepper	**A bouquet garni**	**½ pint fish stock**	**2 teaspoons lemon juice**

2 onions, peeled and sliced   **1 lb. cod or haddock fillets, skinned**

1 lb. plaice fillets, skinned   **2 oz. butter**   **2 oz. flour**

8 oz. crab meat   **8 oz. shelled shrimps (fresh/frozen)**   **1 teaspoon saffron**

Soak cockles in salted water overnight. Next day drain, scrub and rinse well. Place in a large pan, pour over water and bring to boil. As soon as cockles open remove from heat and drain, reserving liquid. Allow to cool slightly and, discarding any NOT opened, remove from shells and set aside. Strain liquid into clean pan, add quartered onion, seasoning and herbs and boil for 20/30 minutes to reduce. Add stock, lemon juice, sliced onion and fish. Poach 30 minutes. Remove herbs and fish. Cut plaice fillets in half, flake cod and keep warm. Melt butter in a pan, stir in flour and cook, stirring, for 1/2 minutes, then stir in liquid, little at a time. Simmer for 5 minutes, stirring until thickened. Add crab meat and shrimps (thawed and/or drained), cockles and saffron. Simmer until thoroughly heated, then add fish and simmer for a further minute.

Potato Pie
Pastai Datws

This supper dish, found throughout Wales, is traditionally served with pickled beetroot or pickled red cabbage.

2 lb. potatoes, peeled and cut into quarters	4 oz. grated cheese, strong Cheddar or similar
¼ pint milk	2 to 3 oz. white breadcrumbs, lightly crisped
1 oz. butter	A little melted butter
Salt and white pepper	

Boil the potatoes in salted water until cooked. Set oven to 425°F or Mark 6. Drain the potatoes well, add the milk and butter and mash until smooth, then stir in the cheese and seasoning. Well butter a 1½ to 2 pint pie dish and sprinkle with the breadcrumbs, pressing them to the base and sides of the dish with the back of a spoon. Spoon in the potato and cheese mixture and rough up the top with a fork. Brush with melted butter and bake for 20 to 30 minutes or until golden brown. Serve with pickled beetroot or pickled red cabbage or with crusty brown bread. Serves 4 to 6.

Welsh Trout in Bacon
Brithyll Cymreig mewn Cig Mochyn

Trout are plentiful in the lakes and clear Welsh streams and this is a simple and tasty method of presenting them.

4 small to medium fresh trout
4 knobs of butter
4 sprigs of fresh parsley
4 thin slices of lemon
Black pepper

8 rashers smoked streaky bacon, de-rinded
2 tablespoons chives, chopped
2 tablespoons parsley, chopped
A little extra butter

Gut and clean the trout. Pack the cavity of each trout with a knob of butter, a sprig of parsley, a slice of lemon and add a twist of black pepper. Wrap 2 rashers of bacon around each trout and brush with melted butter. Place the fish under a hot grill and cook for 3-4 minutes on each side. Melt a little extra butter with the juices from the fish, add the chopped chives and parsley and pour over each fish. Serve with parsley potatoes, carrots and minted peas. Serves 4.

Near Rhayader by Sutton Palmer

Wedding Night Pasty
Pastai Nos Priodas

Traditionally made with hot water crust and boiled diced mutton, this pasty would be served at wedding breakfasts in the Gower Peninsular. Each guest bought a slice and the money raised went towards helping the bride and groom set up their new home.

12 oz. prepared shortcrust pastry
8 oz. cooked lamb, diced
1 large onion, peeled and finely
  chopped
Pinch of dry mustard

1 heaped dessertspoon fresh
  chopped herbs (parsley, mint,
  thyme, etc. mixed)
Salt and white pepper
A little lamb stock

A little milk to glaze

Set oven to 350°F or Mark 4. Roll out the pastry on a lightly floured surface, divide in half and use one half to line a greased 8 to 9 inch, deep pie plate. Mix together the lamb, onion, herbs and seasoning, spoon on to the pastry and spread out. Sprinkle over sufficient stock to moisten. Cover with the remaining pastry, sealing the edges well and trimming neatly. Make a small steam hole in the centre and decorate with pastry leaves from the trimmings. Brush with a little milk and bake for 30 to 40 minutes until golden. Serve hot or cold with vegetables. Serves 4 to 6.

Welsh Rice Pudding
Pwdin Reis Cymreig

This rice pudding is lightened with stiffly beaten egg white and flavoured with nutmeg and a bayleaf.

1 pint milk	**A small bayleaf**
¼ teaspoon ground nutmeg	**1½ oz. pudding rice**
Pinch of salt	**2 eggs, separated**

Pour the milk into a saucepan, add the nutmeg, salt and bayleaf and bring to the boil. Stir in the rice and simmer until the milk is absorbed and the rice cooked, adding a little extra milk if necessary. Remove from the heat and discard the bayleaf. Set oven to 425°F or Mark 7. Allow the rice to cool slightly then mix in the egg yolks. Whisk the egg whites until they hold their shape and fold into the rice mixture. Turn into a lightly buttered 1½ to 2 pint pie dish and cook for 10 to 15 minutes or until the top is golden. Serve with stewed fruit, jam or honey.

This rice pudding contains no sugar, but if desired a little can be added to taste and, although it is not traditional, the bayleaf can be omitted.

Pembroke Castle by A. de Breanski Jnr.

Pembrokeshire Pies
Pastai Penfro

These individual pies, originally made with mutton, are now usually made with lamb.

8 oz. lard   1 lb. flour   1 teaspoon salt   ¼ pint water
1 to 1¼ lb. cooked minced lamb   4 oz. currants
4 oz. brown sugar   Salt and black pepper   Pinch dry mustard
Redcurrant jelly   Beaten egg to glaze

Pastry: In a bowl rub 2 oz. lard into the flour, then stir in the salt. Put the remainder of the lard and the water in a pan and bring to the boil. Make a well in the flour mixture, pour in the boiling liquid and stir well with a wooden spoon until the mixture leaves the side of the bowl. Allow to cool a little, then turn out on to a lightly floured surface and knead until smooth and pliable and still warm. Roll out and line 8 lightly greased, deep patty tins, reserving sufficient for lids. Divide the lamb, currants and sugar between the pies in layers - starting and finishing with lamb and season well. Warm the redcurrant jelly slightly and spoon over. Roll out 8 lids, place on the pies and seal well with a little water. Make a steam hole in each pie and brush with egg to glaze. Set oven to 375°F or Mark 5 and bake for 30 to 40 minutes or until golden. Serve cold.

Welsh Omelette
Crempog Las

As with Welsh Pancakes or Crempog, there are two traditional serving methods; either one large pancake was prepared, spread with butter and served hot, cut into slices, or a number of smaller pancakes were made, spread with butter, piled one on top of another and served cut into wedges.

8 oz. flour	2 eggs, separated
Salt	3 to 4 tablespoons milk or buttermilk
Pinch of nutmeg	Butter for spreading
1 dessertspoon fresh parsley, finely chopped	

Sift the flour, salt and nutmeg together into a bowl, then stir in the egg yolks. Add the milk and beat until smooth. Whisk the egg whites until they stand up in soft peaks and fold into the mixture, with the parsley. Melt a little butter in a thick frying pan and fry spoonfuls of the mixture in the same way as pancakes. Keep warm, then spread with butter, pile one on top of another and serve, cut into wedges, either alone or with Mother's Supper. Serves 4.

For Welsh Pancakes, butter is rubbed into flour, bicarbonate of soda and cream of tartar and formed into a batter with egg and milk or buttermilk with a little sugar and a few drops of vinegar. The pancakes are then fried and served as above.

Cockle Cakes
Teisennau Cocos

Cockle-wives, with their pony or donkey carts, have always been a part of the Welsh coastal scene, particularly at Penclawdd in the Gower. At low tide they would 'scrap' the sand for cockles and boil them over open fires on the beach.

1 quart cockles	**1 oz. butter**
1 to 1½oz. oatmeal	**1 egg yolk, beaten**
3 oz. flour	**Water or milk**
Pinch of salt	**Fat for frying**

The evening before they are required, place the cockles in a bowl of cold, salted water, sprinkle over the oatmeal and leave overnight. Next day, drain the cockles and scrub them thoroughly. Place in a saucepan of salted water, bring to the boil and boil for 3 to 4 minutes until the shells open. Allow the cockles to cool and, discarding any that have NOT opened, remove the remainder from their shells. Sift the flour and salt together in a bowl, then rub in the butter. Stir in the egg yolk, then add sufficient water or milk to make a thick, smooth batter. Heat the fat in a deep pan and using a spoon, dip the cockles, one or two at a time, into the batter and fry in the hot fat until crisp and golden. Drain on kitchen paper and keep warm. Serve accompanied by lemon wedges and crusty bread. Serves 4.

Honeyed Welsh Lamb
Oen Cymreig â Mêl

*A leg of Welsh lamb coated with honey and roasted, served with
cider and honey gravy.*

4 lb. leg of lamb   **Sprig of rosemary**
6 tablespoons Welsh clover honey   Salt and freshly ground pepper
½ pint cider

Set oven to 400°F or Mark 6. Place the leg of lamb on kitchen foil in a roasting
tin. Brush with 4 tablespoons of warm honey and season with salt and pepper.
Place the sprig of rosemary on top of the joint. Draw up the foil to form a tent
and roast for 15 minutes. Lower the heat to 350°F or Mark 4 and continue
roasting for 1½ hours until the juice just runs pink or longer if preferred well
done. Open up the foil to crisp and brown the skin for the last 20 minutes of
cooking time. Remove the lamb from the oven and keep warm. Pour off the
fat from the pan and make the gravy from the meat residue, adding half a pint
of cider and 2 tablespoons of honey. Reduce to two thirds volume by boiling.
Serve with roast potatoes and green vegetables. Serves 6.

The River Dee at Llangollen by A. de Breanski Jnr.

Rabbit with Lentils
Cwningen â Chorbys

An economical and filling farmhouse dish.

8 oz. lentils
1 onion, peeled and quartered
2 rashers streaky bacon, chopped
1 rabbit, jointed
A little seasoned flour
A little bacon fat or oil

1 onion, peeled and chopped
¾ pint lamb or chicken stock
A bouquet garni
Salt and pepper
Pinch of mustard powder
Fresh chopped parsley for garnish

Soak the lentils overnight in water. Next morning, drain and rinse. Place in a pan with the quartered onion and bacon, cover with water and bring to the boil. Cover and simmer until the lentils are tender (about 1½ hours). Allow to cool, then sieve or liquidise. Set oven to 325°F or Mark 3. Dust the rabbit joints with seasoned flour. Melt the fat in a pan and fry the joints until lightly browned, then place in a casserole. Fry the chopped onion in the remaining fat until soft, then add the stock and *bouquet garni* and bring to the boil, stirring. Pour over the rabbit, season and cover. Cook for 1 to 1½ hours or until the joints are tender, drain off the liquid and add it to the lentil pureé, mixing well. Pour back over the rabbit, return to the oven and cook for 15 to 20 minutes. Serve, garnished with parsley. Serves 4.

Anglesey Eggs
Wyau Ynys Môn

A supper dish of cheese and hard boiled eggs on a bed of leeks and mashed potato.

6 small leeks, chopped and cooked
1 lb. of hot mashed potatoes
3 oz. butter
Salt and black pepper
1 tablespoon flour

½ pint hot milk
3 oz. Cheddar cheese, grated
8 hard boiled eggs, halved
2 tablespoons fresh breadcrumbs
Grated nutmeg

Set oven to 350°F or Mark 4. In a bowl, combine the leeks, mashed potatoes and half the butter; season and beat well together. Place in a buttered, ovenproof dish. Make a cheese sauce by melting 1 oz. of the butter in a small pan, add the flour, stir and cook for 2 minutes over a low heat. Stir in the milk, add the cheese and simmer, stirring, until it thickens (reserve half an ounce of butter and a little cheese for sprinkling over the finished dish). Arrange the halved hard boiled eggs over the potato and leek mixture. Pour the cheese sauce over. Mix the reserved cheese with the breadcrumbs and sprinkle over the sauce; dot with the remaining butter and grate a little nutmeg over. Bake for 15-20 minutes until nicely browned. Serve with broccolli or peas. Serves 4.

Penarth: Entrance to Cardiff Harbour by Edwin Hayes

Glamorgan Sausages
Selsig Morgannwg

Not really sausages but a cheese, egg and breadcrumb mixture formed into rolls and fried; a high tea or supper recipe.

4 oz. strong Cheddar cheese, grated	Pinch of thyme
4 oz. fresh white breadcrumbs	Salt and pepper
1 small onion, finely chopped	2 small eggs
1 teaspoon mustard powder	1 large egg
1 tablespoon chopped parsley	Dried breadcrumbs for coating

Oil for frying

In a bowl, beat the two small eggs and add the mustard, parsley, thyme and seasoning. In a separate bowl mix together the cheese, breadcrumbs and the onion. Now combine the egg mixture with the breadcrumb mixture. With floured hands form the mixture into approximately 10 sausage-shaped rolls. Beat the large egg in a bowl, dip in the sausages, coat them with the dry breadcrumbs and fry in hot oil until golden brown. Drain well. Serve with a crunchy green salad. Serves 4 - 6.

Egg Whey
Maidd ac Wy

This steamed pudding has an egg custard filling, flavoured with spices and lemon.

½ pint milk
½ teaspoon ground ginger
Pinch of ground nutmeg
Pinch of ground cinnamon
2 large eggs

1½ oz. sugar
4 to 5 thin slices of white bread,
   thickly buttered and
   crusts removed
Grated rind of a lemon

Pour the milk into a saucepan, stir in the spices and heat until almost boiling. Remove from the heat, add the lemon rind, cover and leave to steep for 1 hour. Beat the eggs and sugar together, pour over the milk and combine well. Line a buttered 1½ pint pudding basin with the bread, buttered side to the inside. Strain the egg custard mixture into the basin, leave to stand for about 30 minutes, then cover with buttered greaseproof paper and kitchen foil, tie down and steam over a saucepan of boiling water for 40 to 50 minutes, topping up the water as necessary. Turn out and serve the pudding with a sweet lemon sauce or with custard. Serves 4.

Cawl
Broth

Welsh lamb is the basis of this substantial meat and vegetable broth; a meal in itself.

2 lb. neck of Welsh lamb	1 medium carrot, diced
3 pints lamb or vegetable stock	1 medium onion, diced
½ lb. peas, shelled	1 medium turnip, diced
½ lb. broad beans, shelled	1 medium parsnip, diced
1 small cauliflower, broken into florets	2-3 lettuce leaves, shredded
1 medium leek, diced	Salt and pepper

Chopped parsley to garnish

Trim the lamb to remove the fat. Place the meat in a saucepan with a very little cooking oil and brown on all sides. Cover with stock and bring to the boil, skimming if necessary. Prepare all the vegetables and set aside the cauliflower and lettuce until later. Add the rest of the vegetables to the meat and season with salt and pepper. Cover and simmer for 2½-3 hours. Add the cauliflower and lettuce to the broth 20 minutes before the end of the cooking time. Sprinkle with chopped parsley and serve piping hot with crusty bread. Serves 6.

Welsh Beef Stew
Stiw Eidion Cymreig

This all-in-one stew would sometimes be used to provide two meals; meat and vegetables for one and broth for another.

1 oz. butter
1½ lb. stewing steak, cubed
8 oz. streaky bacon rashers,
   de-rinded and cut into four
1 tablespoon flour
1½ to 2 pints water
2 onions, peeled and sliced
2 carrots, peeled and sliced

2 small turnips, peeled and cubed
1 heaped dessertspoon fresh chopped
   herbs (parsley, thyme, sage, etc. mixed)
Salt and white pepper
¼ pint cider
½ lb. potatoes, weighed after peeling
3 leeks, washed and trimmed
Chopped fresh parsley for garnish

Melt the butter in a large saucepan and fry the beef and bacon lightly, then sprinkle over the flour and fry for a further minute. Add the water and bring to the boil, then cover and simmer for 40 minutes. Allow to cool slightly and skim, then add the onions, carrots and turnips, herbs and seasoning and bring to the boil. Add the cider, cover and simmer for 1 hour. Add the potatoes and leeks, cover and simmer for a further 20 to 30 minutes. Serve, sprinkling each portion with a little finely chopped parsley. Serves 4 to 6.

Chepstow Castle by Sutton Palmer

Dee Salmon Fish Cakes
Teisennau Eog Dyfrdwy

Salmon is the king of fish and these potato and fish cakes flavoured with parsley and chives are a luxury starter or main course.

8 oz. salmon, poached and finely flaked	1 tablespoon chives, chopped
1 lb. potatoes, peeled	Salt and pepper
3 oz. butter	Zest of ½ lemon
1 tablespoon parsley, chopped	Oil for frying

Boil the potatoes until tender. Mash well with 1 oz. of the butter and mix in the finely-flaked salmon, the chopped parsley, chopped chives and lemon zest. Season to taste with salt and pepper. Turn out on to a floured surface, divide into 8 portions and shape into cakes. Fry in 2oz. of butter mixed with oil until golden brown on each side. Drain on kitchen paper. Serve as a starter on a bed of lettuce with soured cream and chive dressing or as a main course garnished with parsley and lemon wedges. Serves 4 to 6.

Mother's Supper
Swper Mam

A traditional supper or high tea dish that incorporates cooked cheese,
a favourite Welsh ingredient.

12 rashers back bacon, de-rinded   **2 onions, peeled and chopped**
and cut in half   **5 oz. hard cheese, grated**
Salt and black pepper

Set oven to 375°F or Mark 5. Butter a shallow, ovenproof dish and, beginning and ending with the bacon, layer the ingredients, seasoning lightly. Bake for 30 minutes until the bacon topping is crisp.   Serve accompanied by crusty bread. Serves 4.

Mother's Supper is often served with Welsh Omelette, as the two dishes marry well.

Cader Idris by A. W. Weedon

Welsh Border Tart
Tarten y Gororau

This meringue-topped lemon dessert can be served hot or cold.

1 oz. butter
4 oz. light brown sugar
4 oz. raisins
4 oz. sultanas

1 teaspoon lemon juice or a few
   drops of vanilla essence
3 eggs, separated
3 oz. caster sugar

8 oz. prepared shortcrust pastry

In a saucepan, melt the butter and allow it to cool slightly, then stir in the brown sugar, fruit and lemon juice or vanilla essence. Combine well together, then add the egg yolks. Set oven to 350°F or Mark 4. Roll out the pastry on a lightly floured surface and use to line a well greased 8 inch flan case, trimming the edges neatly. Spoon in the filling and smooth the top, then bake for 30 minutes. Remove from the oven. Whisk the egg whites until they stand up in soft peaks, then fold in the caster sugar with a metal spoon. Reduce the oven temperature to 300°F or Mark 2. Pile or pipe the meringue on top of the filling and bake for 10-15 minutes, or until the meringue is a soft golden brown. Serve hot or cold, accompanied by single cream. Serves 4 to 6.

Stuffed Herrings
Penwaig wedi eu Stwffio

Herrings stuffed with a breadcrumb, onion and walnut mixture, fried in butter.
Also a first rate barbecue recipe.

**4 medium-size herrings, boned
and with heads and tails removed**
1 medium onion, finely chopped
2 oz. fresh breadcrumbs
2 oz. walnuts, chopped

1 tablespoon made mustard
Juice and zest of one lemon
**3 tablespoons fresh herbs, chopped
(i.e. parsley, chives, thyme, etc.)**
2 oz. butter

Salt and pepper

Melt a knob of butter in a saucepan and soften the onion. Mix the breadcrumbs, chopped walnuts, mustard, lemon zest and mixed herbs in a bowl and add the onion and about a tablespoon of lemon juice and bind together. Stuff each herring with this mixture. Fold over and close neatly. Make three cuts on each side at the thick end of each fish to ensure even cooking. Melt the butter in frying pan and fry the fish for about 10 minutes, turning them once. They should be tender and nicely browned. Pour on the remaining lemon juice and serve with creamed potatoes and vegetables in season. Serves 4.

Oystermouth Pie
Pastai Ystumllwynarth

The coastal town of Oystermouth in Swansea Bay is not far from The Mumbles,
sometimes known as the Gateway to the Gower Peninsula. This fish pie was
originally made with salt cod and is traditionally served with parsnips.

1 lb. potatoes, weighed after peeling
1 to 2 tablespoons milk
1 oz. butter
Salt and pepper
Pinch mustard powder
Pinch ground nutmeg or mace

1 medium onion, peeled and chopped
1 lb. boiled cod, flaked
1 egg, hard boiled and chopped
1 heaped dessertspoon fresh,
 chopped parsley
A little extra milk

Boil the potatoes in lightly salted water, then drain well and mash with the milk, a quarter of the butter and the seasoning and spice. Melt half the remaining butter in a frying pan and sweat the onion until soft. Set oven to 375°F or Mark 5. Having lightly boiled the cod, flake the flesh and carefully remove all the bones and skin. Mix together the mashed potato and cod, then add the onion, hard boiled egg and parsley and turn into a buttered 2 pint pie dish, roughing up the top with a fork. Sprinkle with a little milk and dot with the remaining butter. Cook for about 30 minutes until golden brown and serve accompanied by boiled and buttered parsnips. Serves 4.

Welsh Cheese Pudding
Pwdin Caws Pob Cymreig

Served at high tea or as a light luncheon dish, Welsh Cheese Pudding can be eaten on its own or accompanied by a salad.

6 slices bread	**¼ teaspoon ground nutmeg**
Butter for spreading	**Salt and cayenne pepper**
8 oz. grated cheese	**½ to ¾ pint milk**
1 level teaspoon mustard powder	**2 eggs, beaten**

Toast the bread on one side only. Set oven to 350°F or Mark 4. Butter the bread on the untoasted side, trim off the crusts and cut into fingers. Butter a deep, ovenproof dish and cover the base with a layer of bread, toasted side down, and cover with a layer of cheese. Mix the seasonings together, sprinkle a little evenly over the cheese and top with a layer of bread, toasted side down. Continue in this way, finishing with a layer of cheese. Warm the milk slightly, then lightly whisk in the eggs and pour over the cheese in the dish. Cook for 35 to 40 minutes until golden brown. Serves 4 to 6.

Sunset at Haverfordwest Castle by A. de Breanski Jnr.

Stwns
Mash

Potatoes and turnips are mashed together to be served with liver and onions, either fried or baked in the oven. This particular meal was especially popular in North Wales in the 19th century and was known as Stwns Rwdan. Swede, peas or broad beans can be used to replace the turnips in this traditional dish.

½ lb. potatoes, peeled and weighed after peeling
½ lb. young turnips, peeled and weighed after peeling
1½ oz. butter   Salt and white pepper   Buttermilk

Cook the potatoes and turnips separately in lightly salted water until tender. Drain VERY well and mash together with the butter and seasoning, then add sufficient buttermilk to give a creamy consistency. Reheat and serve as an accompaniment to liver or other meat dishes. Serves 4.

Welsh Punchnep is a similar dish, but richer. Potatoes and turnips are mashed together with butter, seasoned well and heated through. The mixture is turned into a serving dish and pressed down. Holes are made in the top and a little warmed cream poured into each just before serving.

Apple Pastry
Pastai Afal

Although traditionally cooked on a griddle or bakestone, this apple pie can be baked in the oven.

8 oz. prepared shortcrust pastry   **A little milk**
4 to 5 oz. stewed apples, sweetened to taste   **Granulated sugar**

Set oven to 425°F or Mark 7. Divide the pastry in half and roll out on a lightly floured surface to form two even sized rounds. Spread the stewed apple (which should not be too wet) on to one round, leaving a clean edge. Moisten the edge with milk and place the other round on top, sealing very well. Brush lightly with milk and carefully place on a lightly buttered baking sheet. Bake for 20 to 25 minutes until golden. Sprinkle thickly with granulated sugar and serve at once, either plain or with custard. Serves 4 to 6.

Tintern Abbey by Sutton Palmer

Welsh Lamb Pie
Pastai Oen Cymreig

An old Welsh recipe, traditionally made with the first of the Spring lamb.

1½ lb. neck of lamb	3 to 4 carrots, peeled and sliced
1 onion, peeled and chopped	1 dessertspoon fresh chopped parsley
2 sprigs parsley	8 oz. prepared shortcrust pastry
Salt and black pepper	A little beaten egg to glaze

Remove the meat from the bone and cut into dice. Put the bones in a saucepan with the onion, parsley sprigs and seasoning, cover with water, boil for 1 to 1½ hours, then strain and reserve the liquid. Set oven to 350°F or Mark 4. Line the base of a 1½ to 2 pint pie dish with the carrots, cover with the diced lamb, then sprinkle over the parsley and seasoning. Roll out the pastry on a lightly floured surface and use to cover the pie, sealing the edges well and trimming neatly. Make a steam hole in the centre of the pie, brush with beaten egg and cook for 1¾ to 2 hours or until golden brown. Reheat the strained stock and, using a funnel, pour into the pie through the steam hole just before serving. Serve with mashed potatoes and green peas. Serves 4 to 6.

Laver Soup
Cawl Lafwr

Laver, an edible seaweed collected from the rocks around the Welsh coast, is used to make this nourishing, thick vegetable soup.

4 oz. butter	3 oz. laverbread
2 medium onions, peeled and chopped	2 pints lamb stock
3 medium potatoes, peeled and chopped	Salt and black pepper
1 medium carrot, peeled and chopped	½ level teaspoon caster sugar

A little chopped fresh parsley for garnish

Melt the butter in a saucepan and cook the vegetables until lightly brown. Stir in the laver and the stock, bring to the boil and simmer, covered, for 20 to 30 minutes until the vegetables are tender. Allow to cool a little then sieve or liquidise. Return to a clean saucepan, add the seasoning and sugar and reheat thoroughly. Pour into bowls and serve, garnished with parsley. Serves 4.

Monmouth Pudding
Pwdin Mynwy

In Victorian times, bread based puddings were considered ideal fare for children and for adults with delicate digestions. Monmouth Pudding reveals bold red and white stripes when served.

1 oz. butter	**Grated rind of 1 lemon**
1 oz. sugar	**6 oz. fresh white breadcrumbs**
¾ pint milk	**3 egg yolks**

4-5 tablespoons strawberry jam

Set oven to 350°F or Mark 4. Put the milk in a saucepan, add the butter, sugar and grated lemon rind and bring to the boil. Put the breadcrumbs in a bowl and pour the hot milk mixture over them. Allow to cool and swell. Stir the egg yolks into the cooled mixture and then spread half of the mixture into a greased, ovenproof dish. Melt the jam, pour half of it over the mixture, add the remaining breadcrumbs mixture and finish with a layer of jam. Bake for 40-45 minutes until set. Serves 4.

METRIC CONVERSIONS

The weights, measures and oven temperatures used in the preceding recipes can be easily converted to their metric equivalents. The conversions listed below are only approximate, having been rounded up or down as may be appropriate.

Weights

Avoirdupois	Metric
1 oz.	just under 30 grams
4 oz. (¼ lb.)	app. 115 grams
8 oz. (½ lb.)	app. 230 grams
1 lb.	454 grams

Liquid Measures

Imperial	Metric
1 tablespoon (liquid only)	20 millilitres
1 fl. oz.	app. 30 millilitres
1 gill (¼ pt.)	app. 145 millilitres
½ pt.	app. 285 millilitres
1 pt.	app. 570 millilitres
1 qt.	app. 1.140 litres

Oven Temperatures

	°Fahrenheit	Gas Mark	°Celsius
Slow	300	2	150
	325	3	170
Moderate	350	4	180
	375	5	190
	400	6	200
Hot	425	7	220
	450	8	230
	475	9	240

Flour as specified in these recipes refers to Plain flour unless otherwise described.